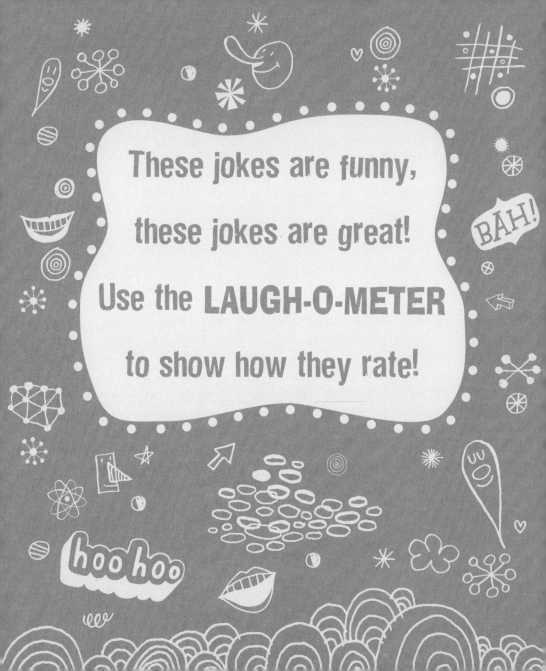

How does the rabbit keep his fur neat?
He uses a HARE-brush!

HA-HA

What's smarter than a talking cat?
A spelling bee!

What do you call a crate of ducks?
A box of quackers!

Why did the chicken cross the playground?
To get to the other slide!

How can you keep cool at a soccer game?
Stand next to a fan!

How do pirates weigh a minnow?
They use fish scales!

tee-hee

What has four tongues but cannot talk?
Two pairs of shoes!

Where do big-city lions live?
On Mane Street!

Sally: Your dog is pretty dirty.
Tim: Yeah, and she's even prettier clean!

What's white on the outside, green on the inside, and hops?

A frog sandwich!

What do penguin waiters say?
"Waddle it be?"

How do you make a hippo float?
Combine one cup soda, one scoop of ice cream, and one hippo!

What happens if a cat swallows a ball of wool?

She has mittens!

Knock, knock!

Who's there?

Bears.

Bears who?

Bears no better friend than you!

Why does the ocean roar?

You would, too, if you had crabs on your bottom!

What's on the table at a monkey party?

Chimps and salsa!

What happened to the dog who swallowed the clock?

She got ticks!

HEE HEE

Why are dogs like trees?
They both have bark!

What do you call an alligator who has too many fun things to do?

Swamped!

What do monsters wear to keep their feet dry?
GHOUL-oshes!

Why is an elephant big, gray, and wrinkly? Because if he were small, white, and round he'd be a marshmallow!

Why did the cow cross the road? To get to the UDDER side!

Knock, knock!
Who's there?
Wooden shoe.
Wooden shoe who?
Wooden shoe like to know!

What hamster wears a tall black hat? Abrahamster Lincoln!

Why does a rooster always look so neat?
Because he always carries a comb!

Why did the pirate become a corn farmer?
He found out he could earn a buck-an-ear!

What do you get when you cross an octopus with an electric eel?

A shocktopus!

Why did the donut go to the dentist?
To get a creme filling!

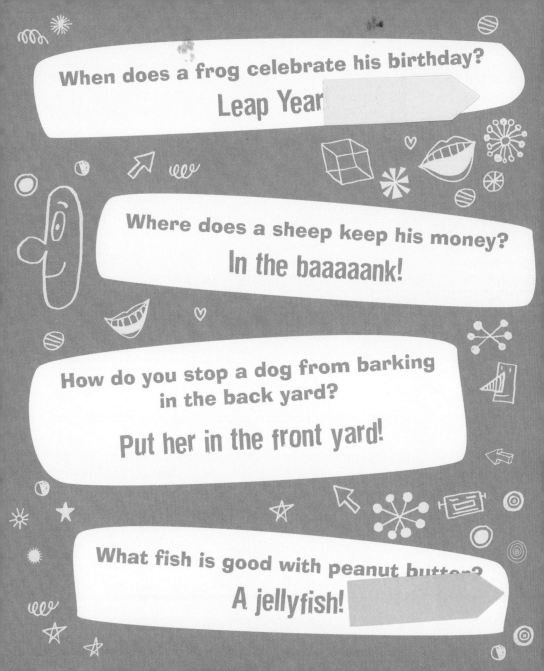

What is as big as an elephant but wouldn't hurt if it fell on you?

An elephant's shadow!

What can speak every language and isn't even human?

An echo!

Why did the man have a hole in his umbrella?

So he could tell when it stopped raining!

BAH!

How do lobsters talk to each other?

They use their SHELL-phones!

What do you call a cow with no legs?
Ground beef!

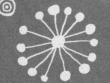

Why did the monster cross the road?
To prove that he wasn't a chicken!

What do you call a frog in your back pocket?
Squish!

How are your feet like your nose?
They both can run, and they both can smell!

Knock, knock!
Who's there?
Boo.
Boo who?
Don't cry! It's only me!

What's an alligator's best feature?
His toothy grin!

How would termites celebrate a birthday?
With a LUMBER party!

Why did the puppies cross the road?
They didn't know the street was ARF limits!

What's the best place for kids who like to stay up late?

Mount Never-rest!

How do pirates remember where they've buried treasure?

They're deep thinkers!

What kind of gum do mad scientists chew?

Ex-spearmint!

Sammi: Did your dog break her pen?

Tammy: Yes. Now she has to type all her letters.

Why did the chimpanzee cross the road?
To say hello to the chicken!

Why was Cinderella a terrible soccer player?
Because she ran away from the ball!

How can you stop an elephant from smelling?
Tie a knot in his trunk!

Why did the chicken run onto
the basketball court?
Because the referee called a fowl!

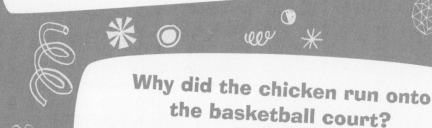

What has four legs but cannot walk?
A table!

Jane: My dog was on TV last night!
Jen: Really? For how long?
Jane: Not very long. I made him get down!

Knock, knock!
Who's there?
Olive.
Olive who?
Olive you very much!

hoo hoo

Where do dogs sleep when they go camping?
In pup tents!

Why did the mad inventor laugh out loud?
Because the rats in his lab
kept tickling his toes!

What's gray, has four legs, and a trunk?
A mouse coming back from vacation!

Why don't sharks ever catch colds?
Because they always get plenty
of Vitamin Sea!

BAH!

Why won't clams lend you money?
Because they're shellfish!

Why does an octopus make a good friend? Because he's always there to lend a hand—or two or three!

What did the mother porcupine say to the little porcupine? "It's not polite to point!"

What do you call a hawk who's afraid to fly? A chicken hawk!

Why are gophers so busy? Because they always have to gopher this and gopher that!

HEE HEE

What's a sheep's favorite sport?
Base-baaah!

Why are pirates so good at basketball?
They have great hook shots!

What do you call a monkey who eats nothing but French fries?
A potato chimp!

How do skunks smell?
With their noses!

What kind of turtle is the grouchiest?
The snapping turtle!

Why do crows land on telephone wires?
To make long-distance caws!

Knock, knock!
Who's there?
Iowa.
Iowa who?
Iowa lot to you!

Why are sheep sneaky?
They try to pull the wool over your eyes!

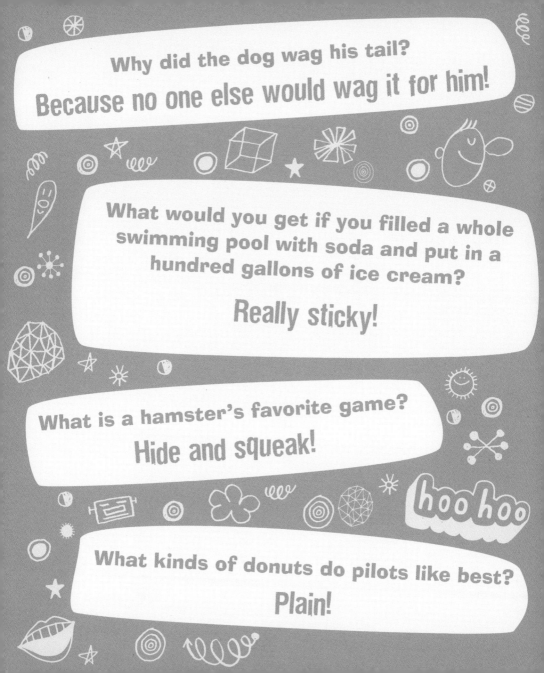

Why do pirates wear bandanas on their heads?

Because they'd look awfully funny on their feet!

Who does an alligator e-mail all of the time?
His pen PAL-igator!

What's a ghost's favorite ice-cream flavor?
BOO-berry!

Knock, knock!
Who's there?
Arms.
Arms who?
Arms so glad to know you!

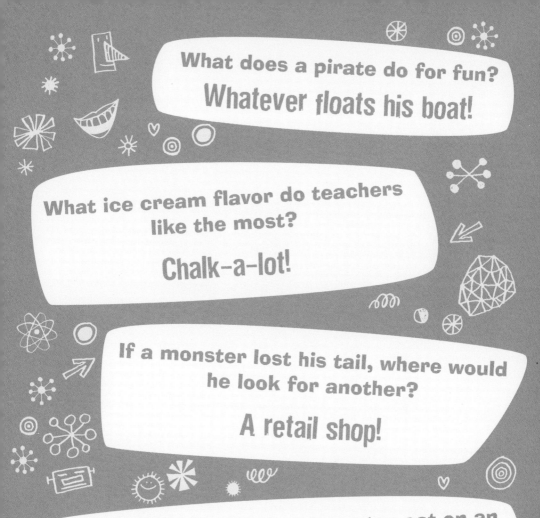

What does a pirate do for fun?
Whatever floats his boat!

What ice cream flavor do teachers like the most?
Chalk-a-lot!

If a monster lost his tail, where would he look for another?
A retail shop!

How many cupcakes can a hamster eat on an empty stomach?
Just one. After that, it's not empty anymore!

Why don't chimps make very good plumbers? They're always losing their monkey wrenches!

What kind of jokes does an octopus tell? Knock-knock-knock-knock-knock-knock-knock-knock jokes!

When fish need to know what time it is, who do they ask? A clocktopus!

What kind of rocket can fly higher than a birthday cake? Any kind. Cakes can't fly!

What do you get when you cross a goldfish and a chimp?

A swim-panzee!

tee-hee

Which candle burns longer—blue or orange?
Neither. They both burn shorter!

What's a donut's favorite dance?
The cinnamon twist!

Why was the ice cream cone such a know-it-all?
Because he always had the scoop!